PLAYING WITH **OOBLECK**

A SENSORY BOOK

BY YOLANDA COPPEDGE

Halo
Publishing International

ISBN 13: 978-1-61244-459-8
Library of Congress Control Number: 2016906046

Printed in the United States of America

Halo
Publishing International
www.halopublishing.com

Published by Halo Publishing International
1100 NW Loop 410
Suite 700 - 176
San Antonio, Texas 78213
Toll Free 1-877-705-9647
www.halopublishing.com
www.holapublishing.com
e-mail: contact@halopublishing.com

This book is dedicated to my son Miguel Coppedge for inspiring me to publish it. To Amira Jones and Terrance Matthews for being awesome students in the book and to their parents for allowing me to use them. To every child I ever taught in my 20 years of teaching early childhood. You made life enjoyable and a learning experience as well. To all the teachers in the world. Without us no one can learn. To all my supporters, I love and appreciate you! Thank you!

Love,

Ms. YoYo

Ingredients for Making Oobleck

Cornstarch, Flour, or Borax

Water   Food Coloring

Instructions for Making Oobleck

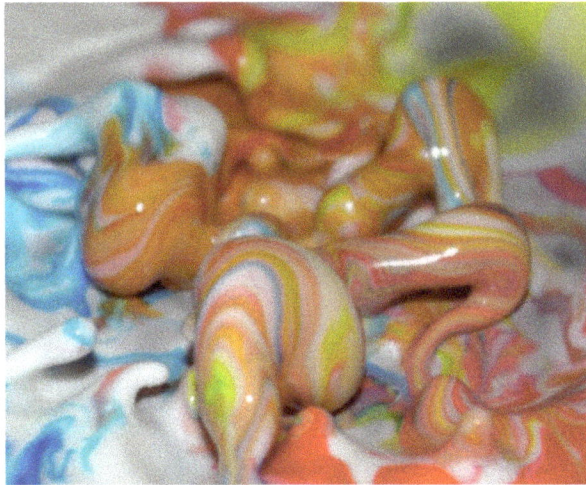

- Start with the water in a bowl (or wading pool!) and add the cornstarch a bit at a time.

- Keep stirring until it has a gooey consistency. You may want to use your hands.

- When the oobleck is just right, slowly add food coloring, if you want. This can be a challenge to get it mixed properly.

- Play with it and add objects such as cars and see what happens!

My hands are white.

It feels soft.

It is wet!

My hands are stuck!

Let's see if the cars can move in it.

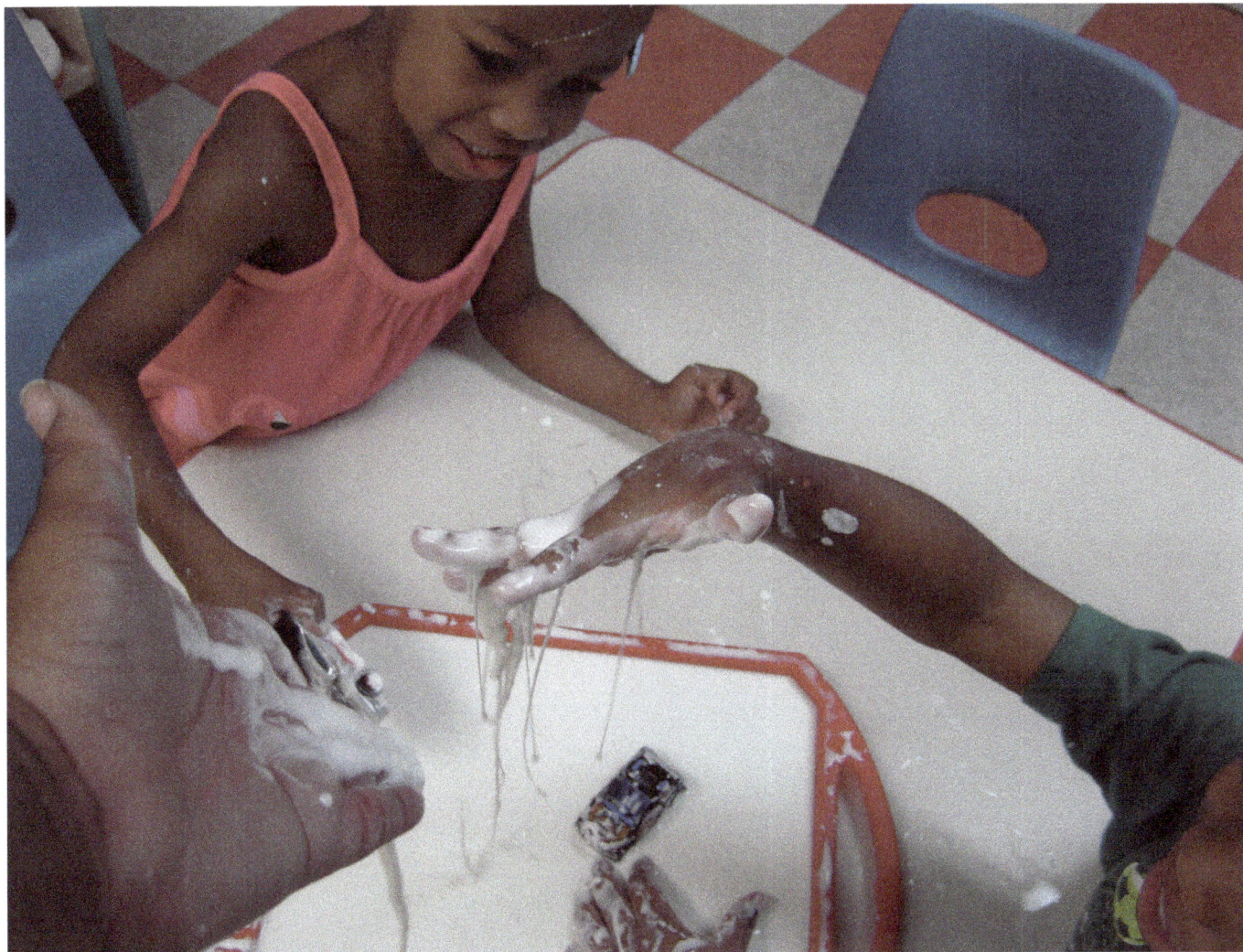

It's slimy.

The cars are stuck!

I got the car out!

My car is slimy.

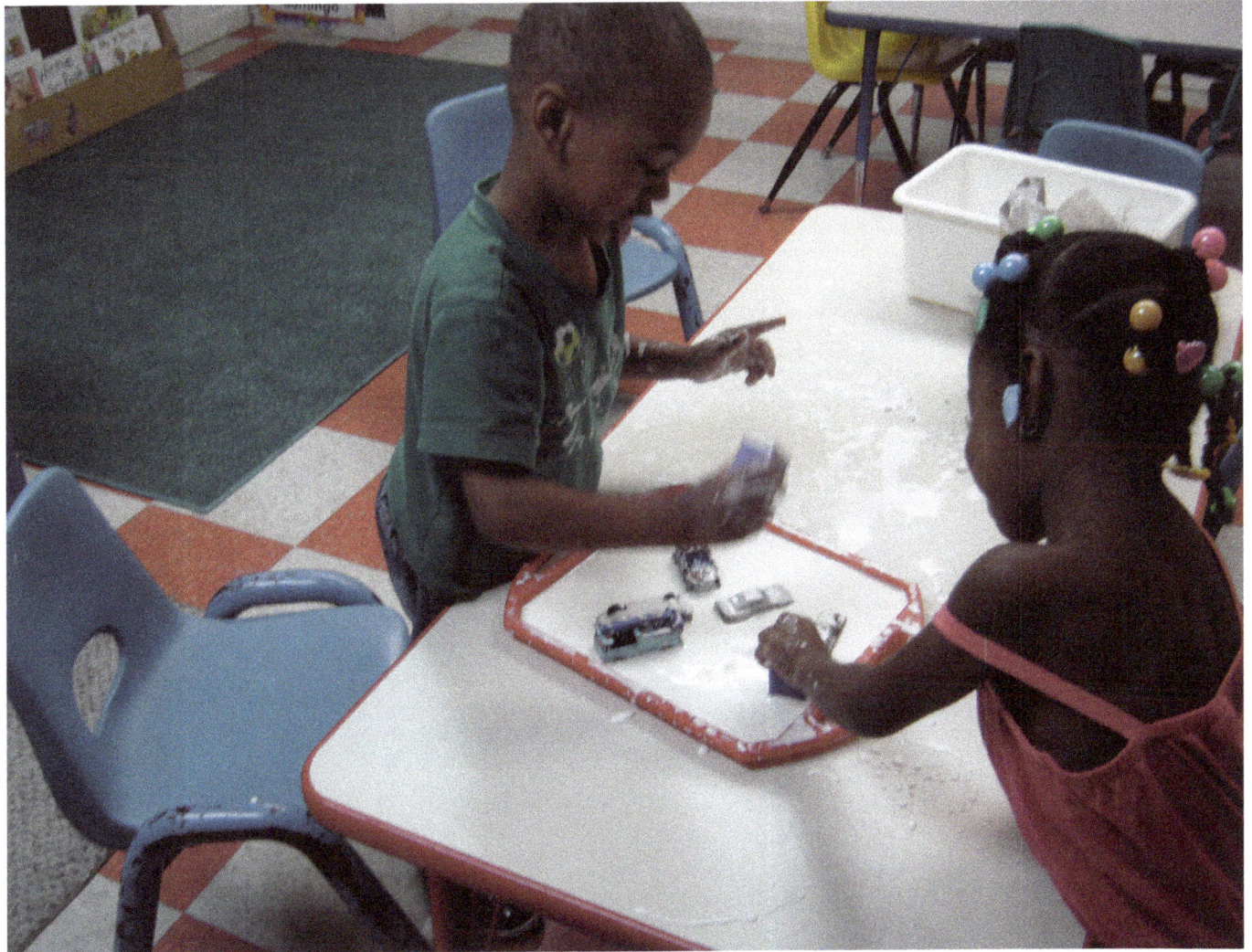

The cars are stuck again.

Let's put the blocks in here.

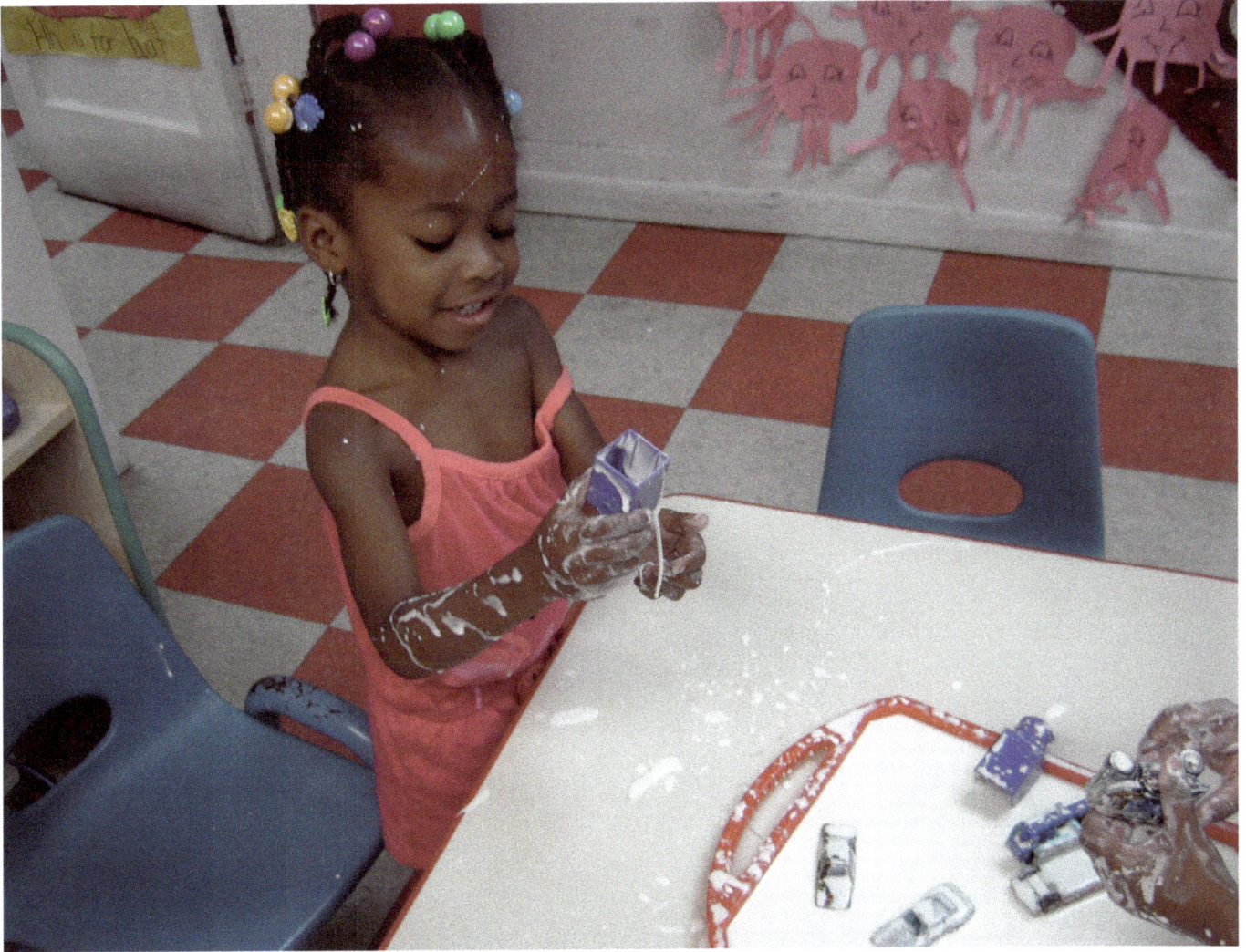

I have oobleck in here.

I like how it drips from my fingers.

It feels a little hard now.

Playing with oobleck is fun!

Other Suggested Books About Oobleck

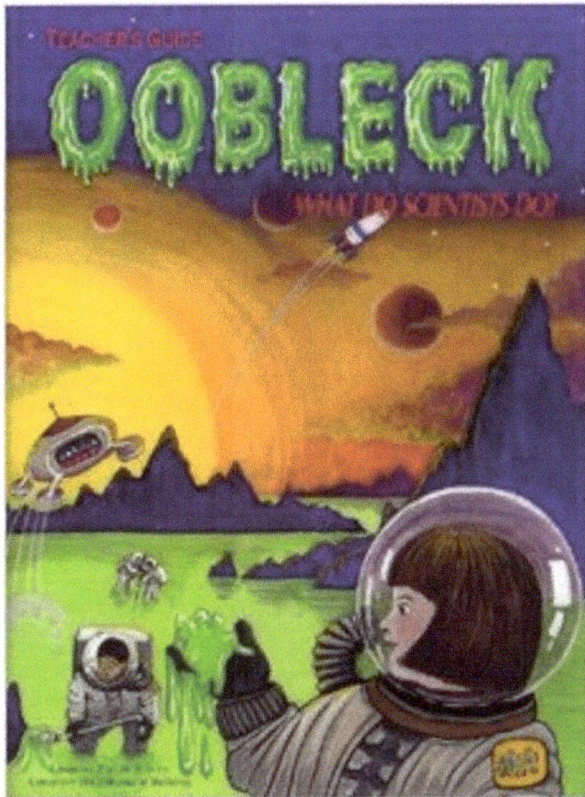

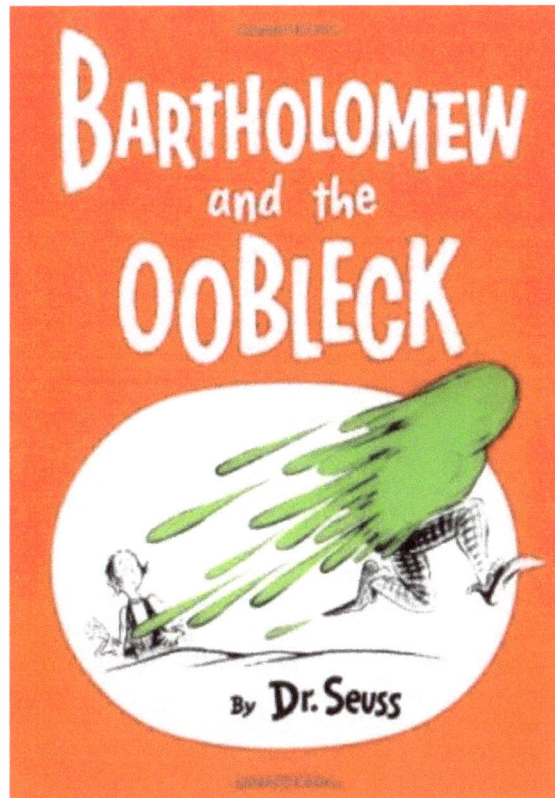

www.ingramcontent.com/pod-product-compliance
Lightning Source LLC
Chambersburg PA
CBHW060800150426
42813CB00058B/2772